Canada Geese

Canada Geese

Fine Feathered Friends

Pauline E. Kelly

InkWell Publishing
Arlington, MA

Published by

InkWell Publishing
Arlington, MA

ISBN 0-9768812-2-5

Printed in the United States of America

*One touch of nature makes
the whole world kin.*

William Shakespeare
(1564-1616)

Contents

Introduction

I began working at an office park near the Hobbs Brook Reservoir in Waltham, Massachusetts in the late summer of 2005. On my way to and from work, I would see Canada geese swimming in the water, grazing on the lawns, and casually crossing the busy streets. I had, of course, seen pictures of them on Christmas cards and calendars, but I was amazed at how fearlessly they would come up to me, and how beautiful they were "in person." Their long necks looked like black velvet, and their markings were crisp, vibrant, and distinctive.

One day, as a group of them gathered just outside my office window, I heard a honk, and then suddenly and simultaneously they all took off into the air and flew out over the nearby mountain. The vision of these large animals suddenly airborne was a magnificent sight, and I was awed by their physical strength and seemingly effortless ability to fly. I felt privileged to have witnessed this avian spectacle right next to where I was standing.

The following spring, three goslings appeared with an adult couple. When I first saw them, they had lost their yellow coloring and were a soft grey color with fluffy feathers. I began to look for the geese every day, and was disappointed on days when I did not see them. I wondered where they were, and if they would return. My fascination with these beautiful birds inspired me to learn more about them.

While researching the habits of these geese, I also heard negative comments from people who thought of them only as a nuisance. Their growing population and ever-increasing presence on athletic fields, golf courses, and office parks has caused health and safety concerns, and has generated a great deal of controversy concerning the best way to manage the impact their growing number is having on the environment.

I am not an ornithologist, biologist, naturalist, or expert of any kind. This book does not offer an informed opinion – only a personal one. It was written from a desire to share what I have learned about these intriguing feathered friends who share our world. It is my hope to provide some interesting facts about these birds, and to perhaps offer a different perspective about them to those who think of them only as an inconvenience.

What's in a Name?

It is the marriage of the soul with Nature that makes the intellect fruitful, and gives birth to imagination.

Henry David Thoreau
(1817-1862)

1

he Latin name for the Canada goose is *Branta canadensis*, or Canada goose. It is often incorrectly referred to as a "Canadian" goose, implying nationality rather than the area from which it originated. The Arctic tundra of Canada and Alaska were its original habitats, but it now lives in many areas of North America and as far away as Mexico, New Zealand and Great Britain. There are several subspecies found throughout North America, but the giant Canada Goose is the most common.

Their native home, the Arctic tundra, is comprised of cold, treeless plains characterized by low temperatures, little precipitation, and short growing seasons. Animals living in this extreme environment have adapted to long, cold winters, and must breed and raise their young during the short growing season of 50-60 days. In this harsh environment, many mammals hibernate during the winter because food is not abundant, but geese migrate south to winter in southwestern British Columbia, the United States, and Mexico.

To enjoy scenery you should ramble amidst it; let the feelings to which it gives rise mingle with other thoughts; look round upon it in intervals of reading; and not go to it as one goes to see the lions fed at a fair. The beautiful is not to be stared at, but to be lived with.

Thomas Babington Macauley
(1800-1859)

Anatomy

anada geese have black necks, bills, and heads with a distinctive white strap under the chin and a white patch on each cheek. The white markings on their cheeks are unique to each goose, and they can be differentiated from each other by their individual patterns. Their body and wings are grayish-brown, and their breast is white. They have a V-shaped band at the base of the tail, which appears as a white semi-circle during flight. Their bones are thin and hollow, which reduces weight for flight.

They have excellent eyesight, including night vision. Their eyes are close to the crown on the sides of their head, enabling them to see close to 270 degrees horizontally and vertically. Their ears are located at the sides of their head, and they have excellent hearing.

Adult males typically range from 8-14 pounds, whereas females are slightly smaller, reaching an average of 7-12 pounds at maturity. The male and female are similar to each other in color pattern. Their bill tapers from the base where it is high, to the end where it narrows, and has lamellae, or teeth, around the outside that are used as a cutting tool. Their legs are close together with very black feet. They have large, powerful wings that span up to six feet. They are relatively long-lived animals, and it is not unusual for a bird to live up to 30 years.

Moon Madness

Stepping out our front door
I'm suddenly awash
in the cries of geese
filling every corner
of the night sky,
silhouettes bobbing
across the lunar disk,
a crowd of shadows
driven to mad dance
by the spectacle
of a full moon
floating free
of the planet's grasp.

Richard Greene

The beautiful swallows,
be tender to them, for they symbolize
all that is best in nature and all that is best
in our hearts.

Richard Jefferies
English writer and naturalist
(1848-1887)

Vocalizations

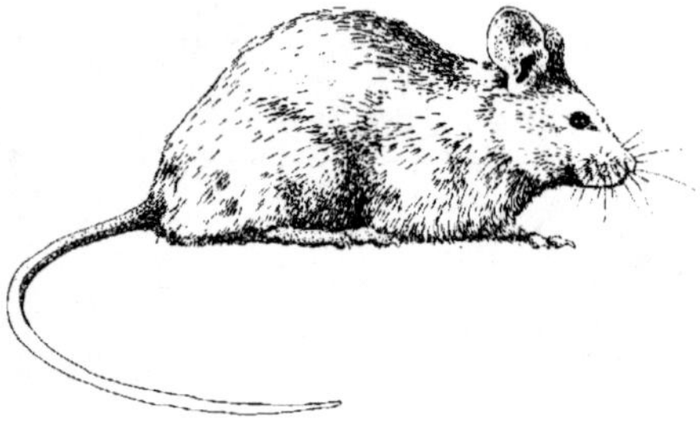

anada geese are very vocal creatures. They begin communicating while still inside their unhatched eggs, with three distinct vocalizations.

The first type of communication, analogous to a human baby's cry, is a high-pitched, long, drawn-out monosyllable that is given in response to acute discomfort. The goslings emit this sound when the egg cools, and it induces the mother to brood. The goslings also cry when they encounter difficulties escaping the eggshell. Later, they use this same cry when hindered by an obstacle, or when falling behind while trying to follow their mother. As with crying in other animals, the call solicits the mother's attention.

The second call, used both inside the egg and later outside, signals well-being and contentment. This multi-syllable call occurs when the cooled egg becomes warmed. If a human talks softly to the egg, it will respond with these comfort calls.

The third call is a "trilling" that is given when the goslings are brooded by the mother, and when they are going to sleep.

The goslings in the eggs also communicate with each other, egg to egg, to synchronize hatching. They will first identify their parents by voice.

Adult geese have the ability to make at least ten different calls. When ready to fly, one goose will give the command, but the goose who gives the command is never the first to leave the ground. Another will lead the way. They make loud vocal exchanges when courting, and "triumph yells" to signify the completion of their marriage vows at the end of courtship. When in flight, they continually honk to each other.

Wild Geese In Flight

The whole world rushes out of doors
When wild geese fly,
Honking their exultations of free spirits,
Worshipping the boundless expanse of sky,
And the resplendent earth below.
Dwellers of earth, following seasons,
Far voyagers: lords of immeasurable space,
Masters of slow moving waters.
What seductive dreams impel their lighting,
arrowhead flight
Into the blue, absorbing sky?
Where do they go; what galaxies do they visit;
What paradises in worlds we do not know?
Free wanderers, bound by neither earth, water or air;
They are the essence of the human soul;
Conveyers of dreams, longings, hopes and aspirations,
Liberated by the spirit, limited only by the mind.
See, when next the wild birds fly
Trumpeting their exultations to a watching world,
If your soul is not soaring with the wings!

Omega Means Starr

One swallow does not make a summer, but one skein of geese, cleaving the murk of a March thaw, is the spring.

Aldo Leopold
American writer and conservationist
(1886-1948)

Birds of
a Feather

anada geese have three types of feathers: flight feathers on the wings, contour feathers that shape the body, and down feathers that keep them warm. When it is hot, they flatten their feathers against their body to reduce dead air space, which keeps them cool. On cold days, they fluff their feathers to increase their insulating ability.

During late June to mid-July, Canada geese, like all waterfowl, undergo a complete replacement of their flight feathers. This molting process takes approximately one month to complete, and during this time geese are unable to maintain sustained flight, which makes them vulnerable to predators. In anticipation of this event, geese relocate to a safe area near water that provides readily available food and also offers long vistas that can alert them to potential danger.

These birds love to swim and bathe in water, especially on warm days. Their bathing behavior looks like play, and they indulge in it most commonly immediately after repelling intruders or after feeding. They bathe by forcibly dipping their heads and neck deep in the water, and then, with curled neck, they ladle up sheets of water. As the water runs over their backs, they reach over and rub their heads in it.

When one of the pair starts bathing, its mate usually follows. After each series of water dips, the bathers rise up and rend the air with a few loud wing-flaps, some rapid tail-shakes, and a leisurely preening session. Preening creates static electricity in the feathers, causing them to repel each other and become fluffy, thus making them waterproof.

Food

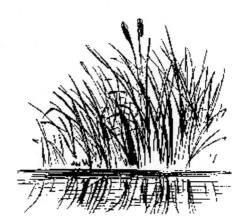

5

Canada geese are at home both on land and in the water. When on land, they eat a variety of grasses, including Bermuda grass and salt grass, as well as wild barley, clover, leaves, roots, seeds, and nuts. They also enjoy grain crops, such as corn, soybeans, wheat, and rice, often just as these plants first emerge after planting, and again when the seed head matures. Geese are able to grab each blade and pull it out with their bills by jerking their heads. They particularly enjoy succulent, newly mowed grass, which is one reason they are attracted to playing fields, golf courses, and the manicured lawns of office parks.

In the water, they feed on a number of aquatic plants, such as eel grass, sea lettuce, sago, watercress, and algae. They stick their heads and upper part of their bodies into the water, with their tail and back end extending in the air, stretch their neck out under the water, and slide their bills across the bottom silt. Early in their life, young Canada geese, like most other birds, require a high protein diet for development. They consume insects, small crustaceans, and mollusks attached to aquatic vegetation.

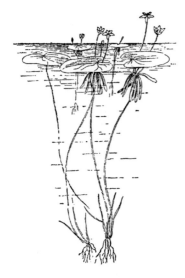

They prefer to feed near water or in fields and pastures that lack obstructions that might conceal predators.

When feeding, goose and gander operate as a team, with only one of them feeding at a time. The goose feeds first, while the gander stands tall and immobile nearby, head high, scanning all around. He first scans in one direction, holding his head absolutely still for minutes at a time, then he turns slightly and looks in another direction, and so on all around. Meanwhile, the goose feeds uninterruptedly without so much as a sideways glance. After the goose is sated and has indicated this by looking up, the gander moves forward to feed while the goose takes over the watch.

When a group of geese are eating, one will act as the sentinal. He will be the one standing tall, with his neck straight and head horizontal, studying anything or anyone who seems threatening.

The same teamwork applies to sleeping. Both geese routinely nap during the day, but never at the same time. As during feeding, first one will nap, and then the other.

Morning Geese

At 7:36 A.M. I heard geese.
The unmistakable honk-honk
demands, DEMANDS, attention.
My shiny new edition of
Elizabeth Bishop: The Complete Poems
slid to the floor, protestingly.

Mesmerized, as though sleep-walking,
I ran to the glass door
and there they were:
changing from perfect
V's into perfect checkmarks
back into chaos
and then back into perfection
and yet back again
in the matter of seconds.
No airforce precision drill
exercise could compete.

Unusual to see
them this close to the city.
Why this place?
Why this moment?

Overcome with emotion
and not really understanding why,
I watched as the last ones
moved out of vision.
I could not express my wonder until now.

The quietude they left behind,
the stillness in the atmosphere,
seemed resonant,
vibrated frenetically,
until once again
the birds resumed their caroling,
the clouds carried on their voyage
across the sky
to India, to China, somewhere exotic,
I'm sure,
and Elizabeth Bishop's exquisite
voice summoned me back
to my reading chair.

Sonny Rainshine

Predators

6

here are many predators of Canada geese, with man, of course, at the top of the list. Throughout the centuries they were hunted for food (and apparently are quite tasty), and then later hunted for sport. More recently, efforts have been undertaken to reduce their population through various methods of extermination.

Among their natural predators are foxes, wolves, coyotes, dogs, raccoons, owls, weasels, and snapping turtles. Unguarded nests and eggs are targets for predators such as gulls, ravens, crows, skunks, domestic dogs, and others.

Canada geese prefer to avoid predators rather than fighting them, and therefore choose habitats that are similar to their natural breeding grounds: tundra-like, treeless plains, free from visual obstructions such as trees that block their view from approaching danger. Their nesting sites are small islands that provide both visibility and protection from the surrounding water. In an effort to be less visible to predators, they lay flat

and still on the ground or in the water with their necks
stretched out, because a goose's head, with the white face patch
held aloft on its long neck, shows up like a beacon in the dark.

But when faced with a predator, Canada geese are
formidable adversaries. They stand tall, hissing and spreading
their strong wings, which are capable of delivering a blow of
surprising force, sufficient to threaten foxes and similar
predators, including humans. They also use their bills to bite
their attacker. And because geese are very social and flock-
oriented, a threatened goose will call out, and other geese will
rally to assist it. A fox trying to single out a lone goose, will
soon find itself facing a small crowd.

Males are more aggressive than females, however, the goose
will protect her eggs or goslings if threatened. If a predator
does get close, she will stand her ground and spread her wings
to the sides to provide a protective shield for her
young. If her eggs are threatened,
she will lower her body onto the
nest and stretch out her neck to
camouflage the nest. She will not
leave her eggs or goslings
unprotected.

Tell Me a Story

Long ago, in Kentucky, I, a boy, stood
By a dirt road, in first dark, and heard
The great geese hoot northward.

I could not see them, there being no moon
And the stars sparse. I heard them.

I did not know what was happening in my heart.

It was the season before the elderberry blooms,
Therefore they were going north.

The sound was passing northward.

Robert Penn Warren
(1905-1989)

Courtship &
Mating

anada geese are essentially monogamous. Pairs form during the winter, during migration, or on their wintering grounds for the next breeding season. Mated pairs stay together for at least one year, often for life. However, if one member of the pair perishes, the surviving goose will usually select a new mate. They reach sexual maturity at age two, but usually don't breed until age three.

Courting is initiated by the male. When he has selected his desired female, he displays increased courage, strength, and aggressiveness in an effort to impress her. He tries to keep rivals away from her, and will fight other males with his wings and bill.

The courting ritual begins with what is known as the "triumph ceremony," where the gander attacks an imaginary enemy. He concentrates on this phantom rival just off to the side of the female. With his mouth open, tongue protruding, neck stretched out and head lowered, he plunges forward,

beating his wings and
splashing water, conquering
the threatening enemy and
protecting the female from
danger.

After defeating the
imaginary attacker, the
gander then approaches the
female. He opens his wings to
the side, thrusts his chest
forward, and moves toward
her with his head down and neck undulating in greeting.
He makes hissing and honking noises. She responds by coming
forward to meet him, slowly lowering her head in greeting,
during which time there is constant vocal exchange. She hisses
and fluffs her feathers, lowering her head in submission.

They yell their loud calls directly in each other's ears, while
keeping their heads close to the ground the entire time. The
courting ceremony ends with "triumph yells" between the
partners. This ceremony is an important ritual that seals the
marriage and keeps the pair together.

If a gander is tempted to stray, and performs his mating
display before another goose, his wife will wait until he has
initiated his display ceremony in front of his new love, and
then, at the critical moment, she will insert herself between
them so that he ends up performing it to her instead.

Mating occurs in the spring in the water. The male passes
his neck around the female's and swims alongside her. While
holding her neck gently in his beak, he climbs onto her back to
mate. The female is usually partially or completely submerged
while copulation takes place. After mating, both geese dip their
heads and throw water over their backs, and then stretch their
necks high, with heads and beaks lifted.

Nesting

hoosing the location for the nest is important, because it must be both safe from predators, and provide open water with low banks so the goose can have access to water plants and places to get in and out of the water. Swamps, marshes, meadows, lakes, and other such areas are among some of the geese's favorite nesting spots. The pair will return to the same nesting place year after year, or near the same place where they have nested before.

The female chooses the site and builds the nest. She often chooses either an abandoned beaver bog or muskrat lodge for a nest site. Such dens are islands surrounded by water. They are usually isolated, but have good visibility, and exclude most predators, such as foxes, coyotes, skunks and raccoons during the birds' most vulnerable stage – the incubation of their eggs.

Nests are very simple and are made quickly. They are bowl-shaped, and average approximately 11 feet in diameter. Reeds, grass, moss, weeds, twigs, needles, and other such materials are collected to create the nest.

After construction has begun, the female rounds out a curve or depression with her body. She drops the materials around her and moves the items to get the best fit. From time to time she will round out the center with her chest or feet.

Once the eggs are laid, the nest is lined with feathers plucked from her breast. Down feathers are also used, as they insulate against extreme warmth as well as cold, stabilizing egg temperature.

Unguarded nests and eggs are targets for predators. Both the male and female defend the nest site until all the eggs are laid, at which point the male continues to defend the nest while the female begins to incubate the eggs. Males defend the territory, nest, and eggs by sending out an alarm by flying into the air and honking when a predator approaches. This alerts not only his mate but other geese nesting nearby. Females lower their bodies onto the nest and stretch out their necks to camouflage the nest.

If predators destroy the nest and eggs during egg-laying, the pair may produce a second clutch of eggs, often in the same general area, however, the pair will produce only one brood per year.

Wild Geese

You do not have to be good.
You do not have to walk on your knees
For a hundred miles through the desert repenting.
You only have to let the soft animal of your body
love what it loves.
Tell me about despair, yours, and I will tell
you mine.
Meanwhile the world goes on.
Meanwhile the sun and the clear pebbles of
the rain
are moving across the landscapes,
over the prairies and the deep trees,
the mountains and the rivers.
Meanwhile the wild geese, high in the clean blue air,
are heading home again.
Whoever you are, no matter how lonely,
the world offers itself to your imagination,
calls to you like the wild geese, harsh and
exciting--
over and over announcing your place
in the family of things.

Mary Oliver
(1935-2005)

The migrating wild creatures...seem to link up animal life with the great currents of the globe. It is moving day on a continental scale. It is the call of the primal instinct to increase and multiply, suddenly setting in motion whole tribes and races.

John Burroughs
American writer and naturalist
(1837-1921)

Incubation

gg laying begins shortly after nest construction. It takes nine days to lay a full clutch of six (one and one-half days per egg). Geese are indeterminate egg layers, that is, the size of their clutch is not already determined when they start laying. Instead, they monitor their nest contents and keep adding eggs until their nest is full. Then they stop laying and start incubation. They want to produce as many, but not more, eggs than they can incubate at one time.

During this time of egg laying, the eggs must be hidden because the goose is not always on or near them to protect them. As long as she is still swimming in the icy water to forage, she does not shed her insulating down feathers from her belly. However, after incubation begins, those feathers are more useful off than on her as a nest lining. Belly feathers at that point will reduce or eliminate skin contact with the eggs, which is required to keep the eggs warm.

Incubation begins only after all the eggs have been laid, so they all hatch within a day of each other to ensure that no gosling gets left behind. Shortly after hatching, the geese will leave the nest, and any unhatched egg will be abandoned.

The goose egg is about two and one-half to three inches long. Its shell is made of protein, calcium carbonate, and other minerals, making it strong enough to support the weight of the goose, yet porous enough for gases to pass through while keeping out dangerous bacteria. The goose turns the eggs regularly to maintain the heat necessary to allow for hatching.

The incubation period of Canada geese is 28 days, which, for birds, is a relatively long incubation. For example, chickens hatch after 21 to 25 days, and most small songbirds hatch after 10 to 12 days. While perching birds are still virtual embryos when they crack out of the eggshell, geese are born precocial, that is, they emerge covered in feathers and equipped with a large portion of their instinctual behavioral repertoire.

Geese Above the River

In the shadows of the evening
Against the cloud-streaked sky
The geese glide above the trees.
Between the darkening hills,
Above the golden, winding river
The flocks skim gently over the water.

Ivy Schex
(b. 1987)

The first law of ecology is that every-
thing is related to everything else.

Barry Commoner
American writer and microbiologist
(b. 1917)

Hatching

atching begins with a rhythmic, scratching-scraping sound. The goslings get to work rasping the thick protective eggshell by pressing outward against the shell with their egg tooth. The egg tooth is a real tooth with enamel, located at the tip of the bill. It will later fall off or be absorbed.

The gosling doesn't peck – it rotates within the egg to loosen the eggshell at the thick end of the egg. After a chip of shell is off, more oxygen enters the egg, and the gosling has direct access to air rather than being limited by diffusion through the pores of the eggshell. The increased oxygen permits more vigorous exercise in trying to escape from the seemingly rock-solid shell.

The entire clutch takes between eight to 36 hours to completely hatch. The process of hatching is called pipping. Baby birds have a pipping muscle at the back of their necks, which gives them the strength to force the egg tooth through the eggshell. Goslings, which weigh about two ounces when they hatch, will be mobile within 24 hours.

The just-emerged gosling looks matted and wet, but it is less wet than it appears because the strands of down feathers are enclosed in thin, horny sheaths that are pressed together. These sheaths are worn off by the goose rubbing her young as they become active beneath her belly. This rubbing results in static electricity that causes the thin down plumes to repel each other and become uniformly spaced so that the goslings becomes fluffy, and their feathers become waterproof.

Goslings are yellow with some greenish-gray coloring on the top of their heads and backs. These colors fade as they grow into the adult color pattern. They all have black or blue-gray bills and legs that become darker as they age.

Imprinting

11

eese have been made famous for the concept of "imprinting," which is is defined as a learning process that is quick, irreversible, and occurs during a very defined window of time during development. With geese, imprinting occurs during the first two days after hatching. At first, the goslings will follow any moving object that makes a rhythmic series of sounds in a certain frequency range. The usually vocal gander is silent during this time so goslings just off the nest follow only the mother, otherwise they would follow both parents indiscriminately. Upon hatching, young Canada geese are able to follow their parents around and leave the nest.

The goslings quickly become imprinted onto the species, but when leaving the nest they are not yet fixated on particular individuals of their kind. They do not yet recognize their parents as individuals, and will follow the sound of another goose. But after the age of two days, goslings learn to recognize their own parents.

Wild Geese

Tonight with snow in the November air,
Over the roof I heard that startling cry
Passing along the highway of the dark--
The Wild Geese going South. Confused commands
As a column on the march rang out
Clamorous and sharp against the frosty air.
And with an answering tumult in my ear
I too went hurrying out into the night
Was it from some deep immemorial past
I learned those summoning signals and alarms,
And still must answer to my brothers' call?
I knew the darkling hope that bade them rise
From Northern lakes, and with courageous hearts
Adventure forth on their unchartered quest.

Bliss Carman
(1861-1929)

It were happy if we studied nature more in natural things, and acted according to nature, whose rules are few, plain, and most reasonable.

William Penn
Quaker founder of Pennsylvania
(1644-1718)

Leaving the Nest

12

After the eggs hatch, the family group leaves the nest and travels together to feed and seek shelter. Both males and females guard their young; the goose will not leave the nest without the gander.

When they first leave the nest, the goslings gather in a thick clump, then follow each other in a chain. They stay continuously within a foot or two of their parents, and if separated, even by two or three feet, they run to catch up. Failing that, in a second or two they summon up continuous long, drawn-out peeps to alert their mother.

The young always stay together within the family in a tight little flock, without any coercion. When the adults get tired and take a rest, the young immediately plop down to follow their example. The goslings are excellent swimmers from birth. The mother swims in front, the goslings behind her, and the father in the rear.

Mother &
Father Goose

13

arenting by geese is unique in many ways. The young feed themselves but can't fend for themselves. They are exposed to predators by running around at a tender age, and although the gander does not need to gather food, he contributes by taking on the role of protector.

Geese have a social system analogous to that of primates. The male parents among geese, swans, and cranes are especially well-known for their long-term commitments to mate and offspring. A male goose makes himself indispensable to his mate by his aggressive defense of predators, and by deflecting the predator's attention away from his family and to himself. He becomes the powerful escort that helps the young survive the many predators from the nest to their feeding pastures. He remains the family defender while the family focuses its attention to almost continual grazing on the open ground where their preferred food, such as grass, grows best.

Both parents will defend their brood for about ten weeks, at which time the goslings will be self-supporting and fully capable of sustained flight. But they will stay together as a family for one year, migrating together, with the parents looking after their young.

What We Need Is Here

Geese appear high over us,
pass, and the sky closes. Abandon,
as in love or sleep, holds
them to their way, clear
in the ancient faith: what we need
is here. And we pray, not
for new earth or heaven, but to be
quiet in heart, and in eye,
clear. What we need is here.

Wendell Berry
(b. 1934)

In nature there are neither rewards nor punishments -- there are only consequences.

R. G. Ingersoll
American attorney
(1833-1899)

Mutual Adoptions

14

eese frequently end up adopting goslings from other parents when families simultaneously arrive at one foraging area shortly after hatching. When families with small young come together, and the young have not yet become imprinted on their parents, then these one- to two-day old goslings initially have a strong tendency to follow almost any crowd. The goslings shuffle between pairs, especially between relatives who visit each other. Ownership of these unimprinted young becomes blurred. If the young follow the largest crowd, then one pair may end up with more goslings than they started out with.

During this impressionable time, the parents are also unable to distinguish their hatchlings, and even if the abandoned parents did recognize their young and wanted to retrieve them from the pack, the foster parents would rebuff any intrusion into their brood for fear of losing a gosling that could possibly be their own. Meanwhile, mutual imprinting would quickly finalize the adopting of the young by the adults, and the young by their new parents.

Adopting these self-sufficient young is not costly for foster parents, because it occurs after the eggs hatch and the young can feed themselves. As a consequence, there is no or almost no competition among the young for food, and there is no readily apparent sacrifice by the adopting parents. There may even be an advantage to having more goslings. The greatest threat to young goslings is predators, but by adopting the young of another family, geese may be diluting the risk of having their own offspring eaten.

After a couple of days, there is little attempt to retrieve lost goslings, as the parents who have lost their offspring know they will be well cared for by the adoptive parents.

The V Formation

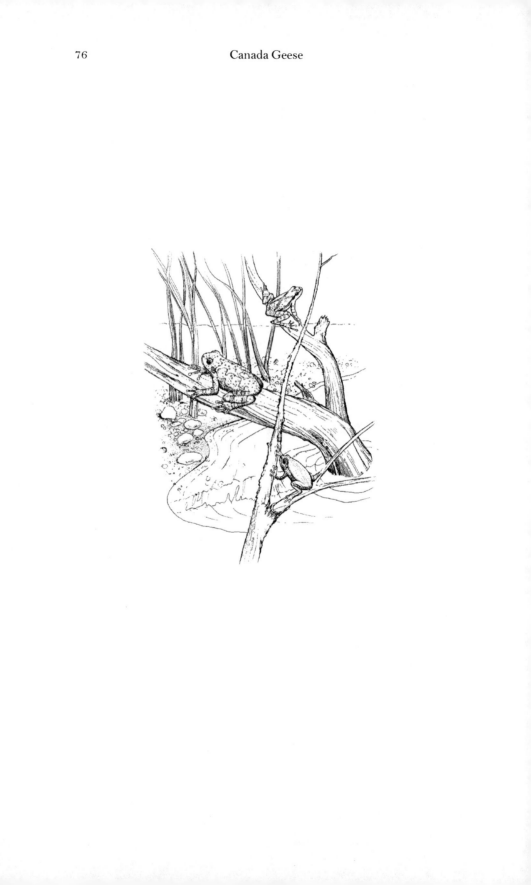

15

he site and sound of flocks in flight have heralded the coming of spring and fall long before humans existed to witness this magnificent spectacle. Migrating geese will travel thousands of miles from their summer homes in Canada and Alaska to winter in habitats as far south as Mexico. Over the centuries, birds that fly long distances have evolved to become aeronautically efficient, and Canada geese are among the most efficient birds at traveling long distances.

Canada geese are strong fliers, with large wings that span up to six feet. They can reach up to 70 miles per hour during flight, and can reach altitudes of 9,000 feet. When migrating, they fly in a V formation, a site familiar to anyone who has heard their distinctive honking and looked up to the sky in the spring and fall seasons. The lead bird "breaks up" the wall of air into which the geese are flying. This air then flows over the rest of the flock, and they benefit both from the lack of air resistance in the front, and the push they receive from the swirling vortexes of air behind them.

It has been shown that birds can fly a full 70 percent further when flying in a V formation than a bird flying alone. When the lead bird becomes tired, it drops back, and another bird takes its place. As they travel, they continue to share the responsibility for being the lead bird among the entire flock.

The V formation also allows young geese, especially those that are making their first long migration, to keep up with the adults. The younger, weaker geese take the positions that enable them to use less energy.

Another advantage of the V formation is that it allows all the birds visibility in front of them, and a clear view of the ground so they can view their route. It also allows them to watch and communicate with each other about potential landing locations. They honk to each other regularly as they travel on their journeys.

Geese use the position of the sun and stars to guide them, and they memorize tributaries, sandbars, swamps, and natural pools of water where they rest and feed as landmarks for future migrations.

A family group will often stay together within the larger flock when migrating. When the flock comes down to land, the family will remain as a unit, and break off from the larger group.

If a bird in the flock becomes injured during migration and can't keep up with the V formation, a few family members or flock mates will stay with it to keep it safe while it recuperates. Only when it is ready to fly again, or if it succumbs to its injuries, will they resume their journey, and look for another flock to join. They will not abandon an ill or injured bird.

Honking Geese, Moons, and Gluons

A gaggle of honking pulls me out the door
into the daylight gray with clouds
just in time to see the wavering vee-
geese flying southward with the sun
past horizon's line and out of sight.
I stand in the cool airs of November's fall;
dry maple leaves red with death
skid across the driveway into piles
then scatter with winds that whisper winter
and leafless trees, bare barked skeletons
hold up darkening snow laden skies,
wordless prophets foretelling catastrophe
that never comes but bring on shivers
of anticipation, waiting for the storms
as geese, swallows and song birds flee.
How Jupiter keeps its moons in orbit,
kept Galileo pressed against his telescope;
in her living-rooted bed Penelope pulled Odysseus;
avian ebbs and flows, waves of feathered fowl
are gluons tying me to earth's rhythmic tilts.

Michael Jenkins

There is no other door to knowledge than the door Nature opens; and there is no truth except the truths we discover in Nature.

Luther Burbank
American horticulturist
(1849-1926)

Migrating
vs. Resident

16

t one time, all Canada geese migrated from their winter homes at the Arctic tundra to warmer climates during the harsh winters, and then returned to the Arctic in the spring to their nesting sites. Native Americans and then later colonists hunted them for food during their migrations, but later generations hunted them for sport, nearly to extinction. In 1918 the Migratory Bird Treaty Act was passed, prohibiting hunting and killing of migratory birds. This law provided some relief for many species, but by the 1950s, the giant Canada goose was believed to be extinct.

In 1962, however, biologists discovered that some Canada geese remained near Rochester, Minnesota, and this discovery lead to a concerted effort to restore their numbers, although less from a motive to reinstate an extinct biological species than to establish a population for hunting. The method they used has become known as "goose roundups," where geese were herded during their annual molt and driven into pens because they were unable to fly during this vulnerable time. They were then shipped to various locations to establish new breeding populations.

When many geese were trapped and moved, goslings were often separated from adults. Some geese were also kept in captive flocks to serve as live decoys, tethered along waterways to entice migrating birds into shotgun range during hunting season. When released from captivity, decoy geese had no knowledge of migratory routes, thus breaking the migratory tradition, and had no alternative other than to settle in areas that were at least somewhat familiar to them. It wasn't until 1935 that the use of live decoys for hunting was prohibited.

Canada geese migrate by following their parents; they are not born knowing where to migrate. Migration routes become imprinted on them while traveling with their parents and flock mates to nesting sites. Consequently, goslings raised in pens have no migratory destination because the cultural heritage of their migration routes and destinations has  been obliterated. And so today man has created a subset of residential geese that do not migrate to their original breeding grounds, and remain year-long in the suburban neighborhoods that provide habitats that encourage them to stay.

The Flight

When the grey geese heard the Fool's tread
Too near to where they lay,
They lifted neither voice nor head,
But took themselves away.

No water broke, no pinion whirred--
There went no warning call.
The steely, sheltering rushes stirred
A little--that was all.

Only the osiers understood,
And the drowned meadows spied
What else than wreckage of a flood
Stole outward on that tide.

But the far beaches saw their ranks
Gather and greet and grow
By myriads on the naked banks
Watching their sign to go;

Till, with a roar of wings that churned
The shivering shoals to foam,
Flight after flight took air and turned--
To find a safer home;

And far below their steadfast wedge,
They heard (and hastened on)
Men thresh and clamour through the sedge
Aghast that they were gone!

And, when men prayed them come anew
And nest where they were bred,
"Nay, fools foretell what knaves will do,"
Was all the grey geese said.

Rudyard Kipling
(1865-1936)

Living with Geese

The light air about me told me that
the world ended here: only the
ground and sun and sky were left,
and if one went a little farther there
would be only sun and sky, and
one would float off into them, like
the tawny hawks which sailed over
our heads making slow shadows on
the grass.

Willa Cather
(1873-1947)

ithin 30 years, the giant Canada goose went from near-extinction to abundance. As its population has grown, so have concerns for public health and safety, centering primarily around fecal matter left by the geese. A large population of geese that frequents a lawn, golf course, or agricultural field can leave behind an unpleasant mess. A well-fed, healthy goose can produce up to one pound of fecal matter per day.

Where resident goose populations are sizeable, the continuous influx of nutrients contained in Canada goose feces can contribute to the overgrowth of algae and weeds in small bodies of water, especially those with restricted circulation and flow-through. Bacteria and particulate matter, when present in sufficient quantity, may lead to the need for special treatment of drinking water drawn from surface ponds or reservoirs. Additionally, beaches and other public areas can become littered with accumulated goose feces that pose a threat of personal injury resulting from falls as people lose footing on the slippery material.

There is no simple answer to managing goose conflicts. Techniques range from non-lethal methods that include limiting foraging areas or eradicating nesting areas, scare strategies to frighten or chase birds away from a particular area, and physical deterrents, such as fences or chemical repellents. Lethal methods include the round-up of geese during their molting season for slaughter.

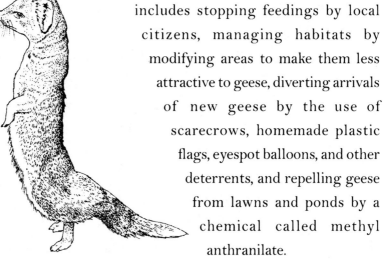

The Humane Society of the United States recommends a combination of non-lethal methods that includes stopping feedings by local citizens, managing habitats by modifying areas to make them less attractive to geese, diverting arrivals of new geese by the use of scarecrows, homemade plastic flags, eyespot balloons, and other deterrents, and repelling geese from lawns and ponds by a chemical called methyl anthranilate.

Geese are intelligent birds that learn quickly and remember what they learn. They are an excellent example of a wildlife species whose behavior can be fairly easily modified by managing the landscape. According the Humane Society, "numerous success stories demonstrate that humane controls have been effective and had led to permanent solutions. Humane efforts require planning and cooperation, and they take time, but they are well worth it."

Naturalist and author, Bernd Heinrich, who studied Canada geese over a number of years, encourages interaction with these extraordinary birds as a unique and accessible way to observe and connect with nature. In his book, *The Geese of Beaver Bog*, he wrote, "the goose's tameness, conspicuousness, and dependence on humans for open and pseudo-tundralike habitats, such as areas of close cropped grass – make it an ideal representative through which people of all ages can experience a close relationship with wildlife, and perhaps reestablish their psychological and physical roots in nature."

Anyone who has ever thrilled at the sight of Canada geese overhead, or who has had the privilege of seeing these magnificent birds up close and has learned about their way of life, knows that geese deserve our respect, compassion, and protection.

The law locks up both man and woman
Who steals the goose from off the common,
But lets the greater felon loose
Who steals the common from the goose.

Edward Potts Cheyney
Social and Industrial History of England
[1901]

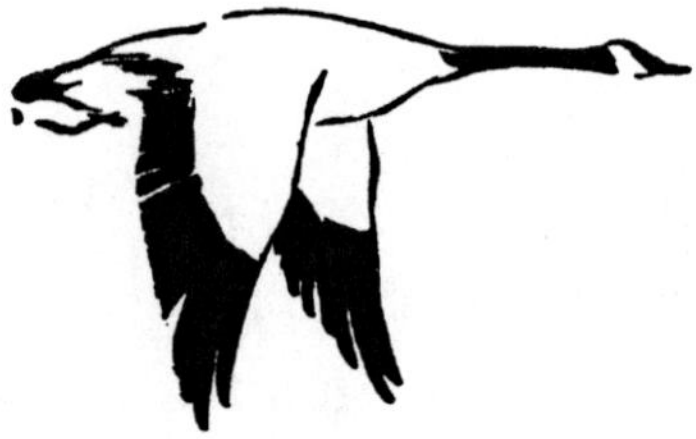

Glossary &
Bibliography

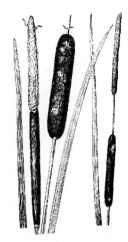

Glossary

Brood – To sit on or to hatch eggs; to protect young by covering with the wings; a group of young birds hatched at one time.

Clutch – The number of eggs produced or incubated at one time.

Down – Soft, fluffy feathers.

Egg tooth – A small tooth on the beak of birds and other vertebrates that assists in breaking open an eggshell when hatching.

Gander – A male goose.

Gosling – A baby goose.

Imprinting – A learning process occurring early in the life of a social animal in which a behavior pattern is established through association with a parent or other role model; to establish firmly in the mind.

Incubation – To warm eggs, as with bodily heat, to bring about hatching.

Lamellae – Tiny teeth that line the inside of a bird's bill.

Ornithology – The branch of zoology that studies birds.

Pipping – The process of breaking through the shell of an egg.

Precocial – Birds covered with down that are relatively mature and are able to move about and find their own food shortly after hatching.

Trilling – A sound produced with a vibration; a rapid vibration of speech.

Bibliography

Bellrose, F.C. 1976. *Ducks, Geese and Swans of North America.* Harrisburg, PA: Stackpole Books.

Bradley, James V. 2006. *The Canada Goose.* New York: Infobase Publishing.

Dewey, T. and H. Lutz. 2002. "Branta Canadensis" (on line), Animal Diversity Web. Accessed August 2006. http://animaldiversity.ummz.umich.edu/site/accounts/information/Branta_canadensis.html.

Ehrlich, P., D. Dobkin, D. Wheye, 1988. *The Birder's Handbook: A Field Guide to the Natural History of North American Birds.* New York: Simon and Schuster.

Grandy, John W., Ph.D., and Hadidian, John, Ph.D. 2006. "Making Our Peace with Canada Geese," *HSUS* News, The Humane Society of the United States.

Heinrich, Bernd. 2004. *The Geese of Beaver Bog.* New York: Harper Collins Publishers, Inc.

Lishman, W., 1996. *Father Goose.* New York: Crown Publishers.

Lorenz, K. 1978. *The Year of the Greylag Goose.* New York: Harcourt Brace Jovanovich.

Robbins, C., B. Bruun, H. Zim. 2001. *A Guide to Field Identification: Birds of North America.* New York: St. Martin's Press.

Van Wormer, J. 1968. *The World of the Canadian Goose.* Philadelphia: Lippincott.

Printed in the United States
70660LV00002B/64

9 780976 881223